The Somerset Coast
Beaches and Walks

Geoff Williams

Bossiney Books

This updated reprint 2017
First published 2011 by Bossiney Books Ltd
33 Queens Drive, Ilkley, LS29 9QW
www.bossineybooks.com
ISBN 978-1-906474-32-4

Acknowledgements
The maps are by Graham Hallowell.
All photographs are by Robert Hesketh or from the publishers' own collection
Printed in Great Britain by R Booth Ltd, Penryn, Cornwall

Introduction

The beaches

Whether you're looking for swimming, scenery, watersports or just lazing in the sun, the beach sections of this book are designed to help you find what you want. Practical information about parking, access and lifeguard cover as well as facilities such as cafés, shops and toilets is given to help you choose the beaches that suit you. Each beach is illustrated.

Somerset's beaches are delightful and safe places – provided users take responsibility for their own safety and a few simple common-sense precautions are followed, especially with children. The Bristol Channel has the second highest tidal range in the world. This means there are some strong currents. The tide rises quickly, creating a real danger of being cut off on some beaches, including Watchet.

Please check tide times, heed warning notices and keep well within the limits of your strength and skill.

Low tide exposes large areas of soft mud and sinking sand on many Somerset beaches. Do not try walking on it. Swim only at higher states of the tide to avoid strong currents. Swimming or boating alone or in rough seas should be avoided.

Warnings of dangerous currents should be taken very seriously. Do not swim if the red flag is flying or in zones covered by the black and white flag (watercraft only). On lifeguarded beaches, swim between the red/yellow flags. In emergency, call the Coastguard on 999.

Other potential hazards that can be readily avoided include drifting out to sea on inflatable boats (never use them if the orange windsock is flying, it indicates offshore winds), slipping on wet rocks (wear shoes) and tunnelling deeply into soft sand, which can collapse.

On a few beaches, rock falls are a potential hazard, but only directly under unstable cliffs. Please heed warning notices. Equally, keep away from cliff edges if exploring the Coast Path.

Seashore Code

Please do your bit towards protecting Somerset's wonderful coast.
    Take litter home.
    Return all live specimens – crabs, prawns etc – to the water.
    Replace seaweeds and rocks where you find them.
    Report anything unusual.

Key to symbols used

🅿	Parking
🅿	Free parking (at the time of writing)
[WC]	Toilets
⌂	Sandy beach
⚓	Lifeguards (seasonal only)
⊞	First aid
🐕	Dogs banned
🐕	Dogs permitted with restrictions (either seasonal or areas)
🐕	Dogs permitted all year (at the time of writing)
✗	Café
♉	Pub or bar fairly near
🏠	Shop(s)
🐦	Wildlife
🎣	Fishing

The walks

The walks section of this book has a variety of routes with great views along the coast and over the sea to Wales, plus many points of interest, including cliff top forts and fossil bearing rocks. The circuits are from 3 to 7.5km (2-4^1/$_2$ miles) in length and can be walked in a morning or afternoon. They are complemented by short and easy 'there-and-back' walks.

On some of the walks you are likely to encounter muddy patches, nettles and briars, so long trousers and proper walking boots are advisable. Take drinking water with you, and waterproofs. Please remember to lock your car and don't leave valuables in it.

At the time of this reprint, work is in progress towards making the 'England Coast Path', which is now continuous between the Devon border and Brean Down.

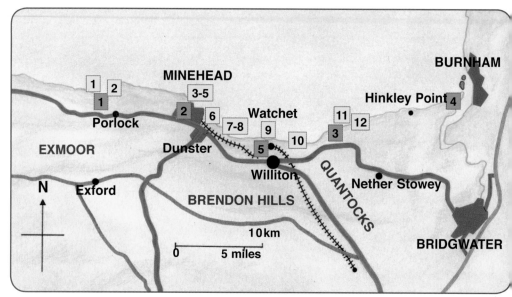

The numbers in yellow boxes refer to beaches, those in green to walks

The Somerset coast west of the Parrett

The 6km long pebble ridge between Gore Point (a 700m flat walk north-west from Porlock Weir) and Bossington is an impressive natural feature in a beautiful setting, a good place to explore on foot (see page 8) but not a traditional family beach. Even more remote, but accessible by hiking the Coast Path, are Culver Cliff and Greenaleigh – two predominantly rocky beaches with some sand at low tide, they lie west of Minehead's historic harbour and old town.

Generations of children have delighted in Minehead's golden sands. Dunster and Blue Anchor are also popular family beaches with good facilities. Like Watchet and Doniford, they are linked to Minehead by the West Somerset Railway, a splendidly restored steam line which is useful for getting about, as well as attractive.

Between Blue Anchor and Lilstock, the coast is a Site of Special Scientific Interest (SSSI) because of its fascinating geology and especially the fossils that are often found. Kilve, with its swirling rock formations and tidal pools, is the most beautiful and interesting beach on Somerset's Jurassic coast. Doniford, Watchet and Lilstock too are noted for their fossils, and Stert Point (page 14) for birds.

Inland there are Exmoor and the Quantocks to explore. See page 32 for appropriate walks and guides.

1 Porlock Weir

Surrounded by woods and hills, this is a place to relax with a drink, or take a stroll to Gore Point (see top photo on the right). The beach has large, smooth pebbles and strong sea currents, so it's more to admire than play on. Go at very low tide to see the submerged forest.

2 Bossington

An 800 m level walk from one of Somerset's prettiest villages. Enjoy solitude and stunning views, fish, or walk a dog, but remember the beach is dangerous for bathing.

3 Minehead Beach West

A long sweeping beach, huge at low tide. It has a traditional British seaside flavour and is well served with shops, cafés, pubs and amusements. The western end is usually quieter than the eastern end, home of Butlins holiday camp. It has some shingle as well as sand and is very rocky beyond the harbour.

4 Minehead Beach East

The sandiest part of Minehead beach stretches from the Station via Butlins to the rocks at Warren Point. Very popular with families, it's ideal for sunbathing and sandcastling. Butlins provide all-weather amusements and welcome day visitors.

5 Minehead – Madbrain Sands

East of Warren Point, it's further from Minehead's facilities, and rockier, so gets fewer visitors, but it has some large areas of wet sand. Low tide reveals V-shaped medieval fish weirs and a submerged forest. Access is from the car park at the eastern end of the Esplanade.

🅿 🚾 ⛺ 🐎

6 Dunster

A huge sweep of sand and shingle, a good family beach with plenty of room to stroll and enjoy the views or stake out your seaside kingdom on the dry sand, where the groynes provide a welcome windbreak. Access is easy – the car park is right by the beach.

🅿 🚾 ⛺ 🐎 ✖ 🏠

7 Blue Anchor West

Blue Anchor is a popular family beach of shingle, with large stretches of wet sand at lower stages of the tide. It has good facilities, including a café/beach shop, a restaurant and two pubs. The railway station at the western end of this long beach is lovingly maintained in period style and well worth visiting – its museum is open Sundays, Bank Holidays and Gala Days.

🅿 🚾 ⛺ 🐎 ✖ 🍷 🏠 🍆

8 Blue Anchor East

Free roadside parking extends to the eastern end of the beach, overlooked by the 17th century Blue Anchor inn.

🅿 🚾 ⛺ 🐎 ✖ 🍷 🏠 🍆

9 Watchet

The beach is tucked away west of the harbour, a 200 m walk from the long stay car park, along Market Street into West Street. At high tide it is reduced to a strip of pebbles and rocks but at low tide it is a vast beach of wet sand and rock with veins of alabaster, extending to Warren Bay. Beware of slippery rocks, rock falls, soft sand and mud if you go rockpooling or exploring. Note, the tide rises very quickly and there is a real danger of being cut off.

10 Doniford

A beach of pebbles, wet sand and rocks accessed via a short, steep ramp from a very small car park, unsigned and easily missed.

11 Kilve

Its chief attraction is its beautiful, swirling rock formations holding pools rich with marine life. Fossils, including some of Britain's earliest ammonites, are often found here. Please read the noticeboard in the car park before exploring and take care on uneven and slippery rocks. The tea rooms are nearby; the village has a pub and a shop.

12 Lilstock

Not recommended as a family beach, but there are pleasant walks on the low clifftops.

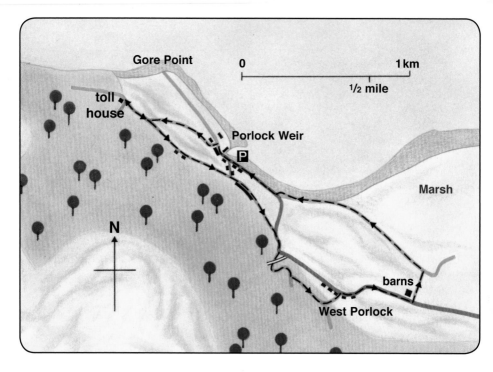

Walk 1 Porlock Weir

Distance: 4.5 km (2¾ miles)

Character: Starting from Porlock Weir – a harbour village of thatched cottages with a pub and several studios and shops – the walk takes in delightfully varied scenery including farmland, attractive woodland, the strange landscape of a salt-marsh and then a stony beach. Some short stretches of seasonally busy road.

Start from the Porlock Weir car park. Turn right, past the harbour, then to the left of a 3-storey building and past a row of shops and studios.

At a fingerpost turn left, TO COAST PATH CULBONE. Climb steps. The footpath runs to the right, along the edge of a field to a lane. Either turn right along the lane for 150 m to see an extraordinary building (a thatched toll-house) then retrace your steps, or turn left immediately along the lane.

The lane leads past houses and cottages with enviable views. On reaching a road, turn right, then after 80 m leave the road and continue ahead up a footpath. Cross a tarmac track onto PUBLIC BRIDLEWAY PORLOCK, crossing a stream.

8

Porlock Weir at high tide

The view over Porlock Bay towards Bossington

At a fork, bear left downhill then at the next junction turn left, BRIDLEWAY WEST PORLOCK. At the road, turn right and walk with care for 450 m.

Just beyond a group of barns, turn left, PUBLIC FOOTPATH PORLOCK WEIR, which leads to the coast path. Turn left along the back of the marsh (the coast path between Porlock Weir and Bossington is a great place to see sea birds on the marshes) then walk with care along the top of a beach of very large pebbles.

After 300 m, climb a flight of steps on the left, then turn right along the road back to the car park.

As an optional extra, a walk of 700 m each way will take you to Gore Point, a quiet spot with lovely views.

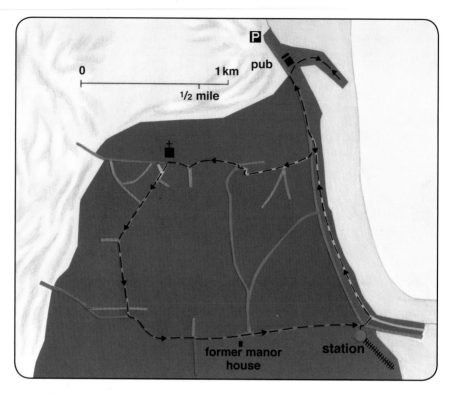

Walk 2 The other Minehead

Distance: 4.2 km (2 1/2 miles)
*Character: Minehead as a resort is largely a 20th century creation, but
this walk is designed to show you an older Minehead – the harbour
area and the village inland around the church, a place of thatched and
whitewashed cottages.*

Start from the West Somerset Railway station. Cross to the seafront,
turn left and walk to the harbour, with its pub, The Old Ship Aground.
Then retrace your steps as far as the sculpture which marks the begin-
ning of the South West Coast Path.

Turn right, NORTH HILL ST MICHAELS CHURCH CHURCH STEPS.
Climb steps then at the top keep right up CHURCH PATH.

At the top of the path, turn left then walk up ST MICHAEL'S ROAD.
Turn right at a junction into THE CROSS. Pass the church, then turn
left down Church Steps.

At the bottom, continue ahead along VICARAGE ROAD, passing
some bungalows then bearing left down WESTERN LANE. Cross a lane,
then turn left on a main road, which winds down to the modern town

centre. Continue ahead down The Parade. Don't miss an old building on the right, which apparently was once the Manor House. The Parade leads back to the station.

Minehead's history

Minehead became Exmoor's main port as Dunster declined. Dunster Haven (now represented by 'the Hawn') had existed from Saxon times, but was last used in the 17th century and had probably silted up well before then. Minehead harbour was expanded by the Luttrell family after 1420. It traded with Ireland and Wales, exporting wool and locally made cloth, and importing coal.

A massive fire in 1791 destroyed most of the lower town, which was rebuilt: the port became less important, and Minehead became a retirement town; then in the early 20th century it was developed as a major seaside resort – served well by its railway.

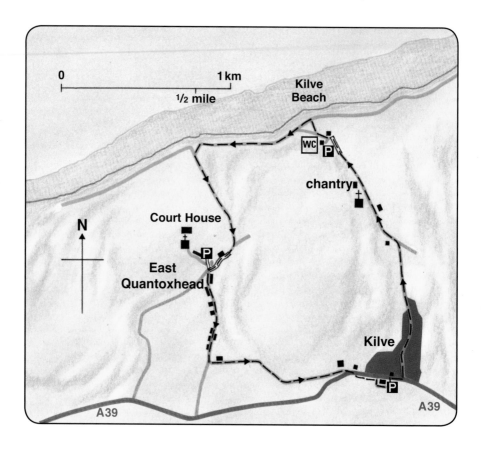

Walk 3 Kilve and East Quantoxhead

Distance: 5km (3 miles)
Character: An easy walk on footpaths and quiet lanes, with one short
section (150m) beside a main road. Kilve beach is renowned for its
geology, and for fossil hunting. The Chantry Tearooms are half-way
round.

Start from Kilve on the A39, where there's a car park almost opposite
the village shop. Turn right out of the car park, then first left down SEA
LANE. After 1km, pass the church and then the Chantry. (Sir Simon
Furneaux provided money in 1329 for five priests to live here and pray
for his soul.)

Continue through the car park and at the far end bear left of the oil
retort (EAST QUANTOXHEAD). Shortly after the First World War, two
companies tried to extract oil from the underlying shales, but could
not make it pay at the oil prices then prevailing.

12

Bear left, then bear right to the beach, which is best seen at low tide when its limestone and shale formations are revealed as wavy patterns. Ammonites and reptile remains are found exposed on the foreshore and on wave-cut platforms. Please note no hammering or collecting of ammonites is permitted and the tide rises quickly. After exploring the beach, turn left and follow the path up the low cliffs westward.

Before you reach the prominent headland called Quantock's Head, the path turns left at a gully, then divides. Continue inland, with a view of Court House, an imposing grey stone Jacobean house, one of the homes of the Luttrell family who acquired the manor in 1207.

Turn right at a junction, EAST QUANTOXHEAD, and continue till you reach a lane. If you want to visit the church, cut across the car park. Otherwise turn left on the lane and, when traffic is directed right, continue ahead past terraces of thatched cottages.

After 500m, just beyond a house, turn left, into a public footpath. Follow it across a field to a stile, then bear diagonally right to another waymark. Walk east across a field as signed and then in approximately the same direction over two more stiles to the main road.

Cross the road carefully and follow the verge on the far side and then the stony path back to the car park.

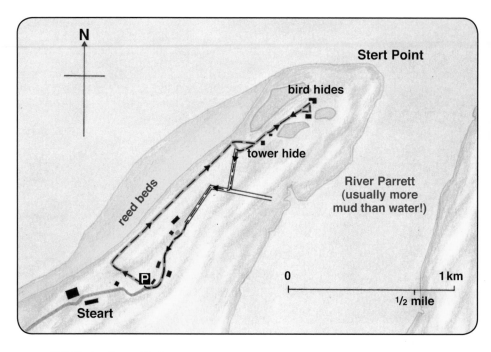

Walk 4 Stert Point

Distance: 3.75km (2¹/₄ miles)
Character: Not everybody's idea of an attractive place to walk, but I
love it for its loneliness and atmosphere.

This is where the Somerset Levels meet the sea, a shingle ridge and
reed bed backed by pasture, where at most times of the day there is a
huge mudscape, with views across the Parrett estuary to Burnham-
on-Sea and to Hinkley Point in the other direction. Even at high tide,
the sea is often a long way off, though clearly it sometimes floods the
saltwater lagoons.

The whole area is part of the Bridgwater Bay National Nature Reserve.
Birdwatchers love it, but the time to see huge flocks is early spring,
autumn or winter, rather than the summer months. The high point
of the walk is literally that – a bird hide on stilts from which a wide
area can be seen to best advantage – and in addition there are four
conventional hides each with a different outlook.

You can reach Stert Point from Cannington near Bridgwater, either
taking the lane through Otterton or that through the attractive village
of Stockland Bristol.

Drive through the hamlet of Steart and park in Natural England's

14

Top: the view eastward from the tower hide at Stert Point, looking over the tidal pools which attract seabirds, and towards Burnham and Brent Knoll beyond

Right: the view westward over reedbeds, with Hinkley Point nuclear power station in the distance

farthest (gated) car park, signed COAST PATH at ST 275460.

Leave by the permissive path. When you reach the shingle bank, turn right along the path. (Some people may find the pebbles hard to walk on: if so, return to the car park and use the return route for a there-and-back walk.)

When the path ends, cross a field to the tower hide, from which a path leads on as far as a double hide. For your return, bear left at the hide-on-stilts to a gateway, and follow a track. After turning right, then left, it becomes a tarmac lane at Manor Farm, and leads back to the car park.

Walk 5 Watchet

This short there-and-back walk includes great views of Watchet, the Brendon Hills and the Coast at the cost of some uphill work. With luck you'll also have a good view of a passing steam or vintage diesel train.

Turn left out of Watchet's long stay car park near the harbour. Turn left again 50 m ahead, OLD MINERAL LINE. Follow MILL LANE past the Star Inn and the Royal British Legion. Branch right into WHITEHALL. When the road curves left, continue ahead, OLD MINERAL LINE, past houses to a path division. Turn right just before a railway bridge (BLUE ANCHOR ROAD – sign obscured at the time of writing).

Cross a stile and follow the path steeply uphill away from the railway. Listen out for trains! Cross another stile and follow the path ahead uphill, keeping the hedge on your right. Cross a further stile and follow the path steadily uphill to the road. Turn right and follow the road downhill for 150 m. Turn left up steps at the waymark.

Follow the coastal path uphill past Daw's Castle to enjoy the views. Daw's Castle is a coastal fort possibly dating from the Iron Age and certainly refortified in Saxon times against Viking raids. Follow the Coast Path downhill to visit Warren Beach. Turn right at the path junction in the caravan park, down a concrete track.

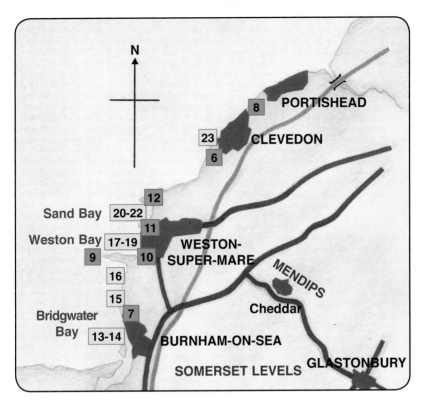

The numbers in yellow boxes refer to beaches, those in green to walks

The Somerset coast north of the Parrett

Three large bays dominate the coast between the river Parrett and Sand Point and hold some of Somerset's most popular family beaches. Each bay forms a long beach of golden sand, with several entry points: Bridgwater Bay contains Burnham-on-Sea, Berrow and Brean beaches; Weston Bay has Weston-Super-Mare and Uphill beaches; whilst Sand Bay stretches from Worlebury through Kewstoke to Sand Point.

Impressive rocky headlands separate each bay from its neighbour and make ideal short walks (see pages 26-29). Brean Down divides Bridgwater Bay from Weston Bay and provides spectacular views of both. Worlebury, with its large Iron Age fort, guards Weston Bay and Middle Hope overlooks both Sand Bay and the coast northwards.

Inland there is the fascinating drained marshland area known as the Somerset Levels to explore, as well as the Mendip hills, with Cheddar Gorge. See page 32 for walks and guidebooks.

13 Burnham South

A seaside resort with a vast beach easily accessed by a ramp and acres of dry sand for sunbathing and sandcastling. Paddling and swimming are possible at high tide, but low tide uncovers soft mud and sinking sand, making it dangerous to approach the water. Dogs 🐕 all year on the main beach, but 🐕 off-season at the south end.

🅿 🚾 ⛺ 🎣 ✕ 🍷 🏠

14 Burnham North

From Burnham to Brean there are 10km of continuous beach to explore at low tide, but soft muds and rapid tides make conditions treacherous beyond the hard sand.

🅿 🚾 ⛺ 🎣 🐕 ✕ 🍷 🏠

15 Berrow

A vast beach of both dry and wet sand, with soft sand and mud at low tide, when it is dangerous to approach the water. Warden patrolled, it is ideal for exercising dogs and horses. The Nature Reserve is remarkable for birds, butterflies and maritime plants. The dunes are surprisingly secluded. Nearby Brean village has facilities and amusements aplenty.

🅿 🅿 🚾 ⛺ 🐕

16 Brean

Brean Cove at the northern end of the Berrow road is less busy than Brean village, with direct access to the beach as well as Brean Down. There is sometimes beach parking on Brean Beach.

🅿 🚾 ⛺ 🐕 ✕ 🍷 🏠

17 Uphill

At the southern end of Weston Bay, this draws far fewer visitors than Weston itself. Its beach is a continuation of Weston's and has the same characteristics: a broad stretch of golden sand (parking permitted), with soft mud at lower stages of the tide. It is also the start of the Weston Wind Zone, reserved for parakarting, sailkarting and related sports. Uphill village has pubs and a restaurant.

18 Weston South (Clifton Sands)

A huge beach of golden sand complemented by a range of facilities and attractions: donkey rides, an aquarium, marine lake, beach swings, etc. The Grand Pier was rebuilt after being destroyed by fire in 2008. With beach parking and wheelchair ramps onto the sands, Weston's beach is very accessible and is carefully managed by a team of rangers. Dogs 🐕 on main beach, but 🐕 at the far end of the beach.

19 Weston North (Knightstone)

The Weston Wheel, Winter Gardens, Sea Aquarium and Grand Pier are towards the northern end of Weston's long beach. There are great views to Brean Down, Worlebury and over the Bristol Channel to Wales. Avoid the dangerous mud at low tide. Dogs 🐕 May-September on main beach, but 🐕 at the far ends.

19

20 Sand Bay South

Sand Bay is quieter and less developed than either Weston Bay or Bridgwater Bay. Its southern tip has some rock and pebbles, but a short walk over the dunes leads to a long beach of golden sand – with a huge stretch of mud at low tide. There is a pub in Kewstoke and a tearoom in Sand Bay.

P △ ↖ ✕

21 Sand Bay Central

The sandiest part of Sand Bay's 2.5km long beach is the middle, though there is some shingle mixed in. As at the southern end, parking is free and access easy over the dunes.

P ᵂᶜ △ ↖ ✕

22 Sand Bay North

The National Trust car park at the northern end of Beach Road gives access to walks over Middle Hope and the nature reserve. The *very* small pebble and rock beach is a 500m walk via an easy, level path beside the saltmarsh.

P ᵂᶜ ↖ ⤷

23 Clevedon Beach

Clevedon has two small shingle beaches, one by the pier and one by the marine lake, built for swimming and model boats. Easy access, good facilities and nearby parking are their main assets. There is also a remoter and quieter shingle beach at Layde Bay, just north of town. Approached by steps, it has no facilities, but free parking.

P P ᵂᶜ ↖ ✕ ⍾ ⌂

20

Walk 6   Clevedon

Starting from Clevedon's restored pier (1869), this 2.4km (1 1/2 mile) each way walk follows Clevedon's sea front before making a gentle ascent of Wain's Hill via the Poet's Walk for some stunning views.

Park on the sea front near Clevedon Pier, or at Salthouse Fields car park. A pier ticket gives access to the Pagoda Tearoom at the end of the Pier, where the viewing table explains the vista from Sand Point to Flat Holm, Cardiff, the Brecon Beacons and the newer Severn Bridge. Facing the Pier, turn left and follow the sea front past the beach and Heritage Centre, which illustrates Clevedon's development as a seaside resort, with period photographs and drawings.

Continue along the sea front POET'S WALK, so called because Coleridge lived briefly in Clevedon, Tennyson's great friend Arthur Hallam was buried at St Andrew's (below) and Thackeray was often a guest at nearby Clevedon Court. Follow the sea front past the 1887 bandstand opposite Salthouse Fields car park. Continue past another small beach and the marine lake. Climb steps (POET'S WALK) and turn right along the tarmac path. Divert left (ST ANDREW'S CHURCH), or continue along the path to see the site of the hillfort on Wain Hill and enjoy the views.

21

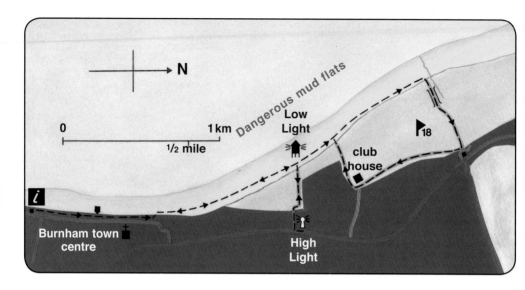

Walk 7 Burnham on Sea

Distance: 6.3 km (4 miles) plus a 1 km diversion to see the High Light.
Character: Starting with a walk along the sands, then making a
circuit of the golf course, this easy and agreeable walk features all three
Burnham lighthouses.

NB This is not a walk you can do at high tide, and at any stage of the
tide you need to be aware that the sand and mud are treacherous. It is
possible to sink in and be trapped, waiting for the tide to come in...

Start from the Esplanade and head north, passing the Pavilion and
then St Andrew's Church, which, strangely, contains two huge angel
statues and an altarpiece featuring cherubs, all carved for James II's
Whitehall Palace by Grinling Gibbons – in a style which later royals
presumably disliked, because they sold it off.

Just beyond the church, descend to the sands and walk to the lighthouse on stilts (the Low Lighthouse). Continue along the sand for
1 km, and you will find a path leading inland.

Cross the dunes, then some boggy ground by a wooden pathway,
and finally cross the golf course – beware of flying golf balls. Turn
right along the far edge of the golf course, into an enclosed path and
follow it past the Club House, after which it turns right, back out to
the beach.

If you have time and energy, take a diversion (500 m each way) to
see the High Lighthouse: a path inland just beyond the Low Light

gives you a good view of it.

Returning to the beach, turn left back to Burnham, and ascend the steps to the Esplanade. On a building just before the church, you can see the stump of a round tower, which was the original lighthouse.

The Burnham lights

The shifting sands of the Parrett estuary are extremely difficult to navigate and the lighthouses have been crucial. There is a folklore version of how the first light was built, but it is more likely that a light was first maintained on the church tower, and then in the late eighteenth century the vicar raised a subscription to build a single round tower lighthouse, later taken over by Trinity House.

A new survey of the Bristol Channel led to the Low and High Lights being built simultaneously in 1834, and the old tower shortened to a stump. A vessel approaching Bridgwater Bar could line up either the lights or the red lines painted on their seaward sides, and follow a safe course – except that within ten years the sands had shifted again! Today the Low Light is operational, but the High Lighthouse is used for holiday lets.

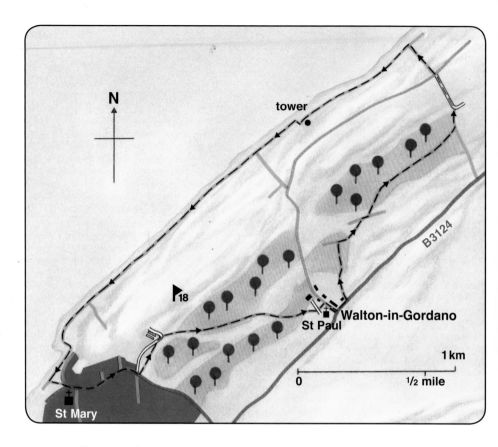

Walk 8 Walton-in-Gordano

Distance: 7.5km (4¹/₂ miles)

Character: A stretch of coastal path is preceded by an attractive inland walk on footpaths – across a golf course where you will see more woodland than fairways (but do take care) then across Walton Common, which is mostly woodland but with some open glades, then farmland. An excellent shady walk on a hot day.

Find on-street parking near St Mary's Church, Walton-St-Mary, which is at the northern end of Clevedon. From the church, walk up CASTLE ROAD.

Take the third on the left, a private road into the golf club, signed PUBLIC FOOTPATH. Almost immediately turn right through a gate into the footpath. At Tee 17 continue ahead up the tarmac drive, passing a terrace of cottages on your left, then continue ahead on a rougher track.

Fork left and go through a kissing gate. Ignore tracks and paths to either side. The path enters woodland then descends, crossing further fairways and patches of woodland, bringing you to St Paul's church, Walton-in-Gordano. Walk through the churchyard and turn right along the lane.

At the crossroads turn left and follow the pavement for 90m, then turn left on PUBLIC FOOTPATH. Cross two fields (stiles) and enter woodland. Climb quite steeply to a path crossing and turn right.

Join another track, then shortly bear left into more woodland. At a T-junction of tracks, turn left out of the woods and walk out to a road. Cross directly over (PUBLIC FOOTPATH). Descend a field with the hedge on your left then cross a stile, which will bring you to the coast path. Turn left.

Follow the coast path for nearly 3km. Eventually it reaches a street on the left. Continue on the path parallel to the street, past a circular building, then turn sharp left up a path, initially tarmac.

Continue to the top, where you will see St Mary's Church across the road.

On the top of Brean Down, looking towards Weston-super-Mare

Suggestions for there-and-back walks

Walk 9 Brean Down

Brean Down provides dramatic views in all directions and has a Victorian fort to explore. Thrust like a great natural pier into the Bristol Channel, this dramatic limestone outlier of the Mendips is also a nature reserve, rich in butterflies, rare plants and birds. All on footpaths, the walk calls for one short, sharp climb and descent.

Please keep dogs on leads because of the steep cliffs, the grazing cattle and goats, and to protect nesting birds.

Take the signed public footpath at the north end of Brean Down's National Trust car park. Follow it up the steep, stepped path to the left of the bird gardens. At the top of the steps, turn left and follow the well beaten path over the turf. Walk past the triangulation pillar (97 m/318 ft) and on to Brean Down Fort.

One of a series of 'Palmerston Forts' around the coast, designed to protect Britain against the resurgent power of France, Brean fort was completed in 1870 and armed with seven 7 inch muzzle-loading rifled cannons in 1877. Each had a range of three miles – sufficient to cover the batteries at Steep Holm.

Walk 10 Uphill

This level walk includes some fine views as well as Uphill beach and saltmarsh, noted for birds. Uphill is just south of Weston-super-Mare. Use the parking area near Uphill marina, or the parking area between

Uphill Marina, overlooked by the church on the cliff

Uphill church and Uphill marina (the old quarry) if this is full.

With your back to the marina entrance, walk ahead 50m to a bus stop. Turn left and follow the unsigned concrete path ahead. Continue on the raised embankment through a wooden gate. A creek and the marina are on your left, overlooked by Uphill church.

When the path divides, turn right away from the marina and follow the path through the saltmarsh to the River Axe. Turn right and follow the river to the beach. You can loop back to the start by following the sea wall. When the wall ends, turn right into LINKS ROAD and follow it back to the marina.

Walk 11 Worlebury Hill

An Iron Age hillfort with high stone ramparts is a special feature of this woodland walk. Worlebury Hill is crisscrossed with paths, but the most direct and level path to the hillfort from the parking area at the end of WORLEBURY HILL ROAD is the one built for wheelchair access.

It is 1.6km (1 mile) long and begins beside a rough track through mature woodland, past a children's adventure playground to a picnic area by the water tower. Follow the path to the hillfort.

Just beyond the hillfort, there is a glade on the right giving a great view northwards. Look around for circular pits. Cut two metres into the solid rock, these were probably dug as grain storage pits – and 93 of them have been discovered. However, they were found to contain a mass of human skeletons that had been hacked and gashed. This suggests they belonged to victims of an attack on the hillfort.

Woodland at Worlebury Hill

The view over Sand Point at Middle Hope

Walk 12   Middle Hope

Study the helpful information board and map at the entrance to the National Trust car park at the northern end of Sand Bay before starting. It explains Middle Hope's main points of interest: the Iron Age hillfort, its birds and butterflies and its geology. As the map shows, a variety of walks are possible.

For the hillfort and Sand Point (1.2 km or ¾ mile), climb the steps in front of you. Keep left at the top of the steps and continue steadily uphill to the triangulation pillar. The mound ahead is the centre of the hillfort. The path continuing on to Sand Point is rather uneven, but the panorama, including Sand Bay, Birnbeck Pier, Steep Holm (the island on the left) and Flat Holm (with its foghorn station), South Wales and the Bristol Channel is excellent.

Somerset's Harbours

Minehead Harbour

'The best port and safest harbour in Somerset' was Daniel Defoe's judgment of Minehead's stone built harbour. Surrounded by attractive 17th and 18th century houses that reflect the heyday of its sea trade, it nowadays shelters fishing boats, pleasure craft and yachts. *Waverley*, the world's last ocean-going paddle steamer, makes summer trips from here. The lifeboat station with its two rescue boats and launching tractor is open to the public.

Watchet Harbour

Watchet's attractive harbour is a marina today, but it has a long commercial history. As the information board explains, Watchet is pre-Conquest in origin and grew into a prosperous medieval town with a cloth industry and market. You can find out more about Watchet's maritime and industrial past at the excellent harbourside museum (open daily 10.30-4.30 in season), or take a stroll along the quay.

There is a sculpture of Yankee Jack, a Watchet shantyman, and another of the Ancient Mariner. Samuel Taylor Coleridge wrote 'The Rime of the Ancient Mariner' when he lived nearby at Nether Stowey on the Quantock Hills and explored the Somerset and North Devon coasts with William and Dorothy Wordsworth. He may well have had Watchet in mind in describing the harbour in the poem.

Bridgwater's quays are no longer used for commerce, but West Quay retains a line of distinctive buildings to remind visitors of a vanished era

The Canal Basin at Bridgwater

Bridgwater Quay and Canal Basin

Bridgwater reached its zenith as a port in the 14th century, when the river Parrett was deep enough for the small sea-going ships of the age to reach the town's quays. Goods were carried upriver far inland to Langport, the limit of the Parrett's tidal reach, and even beyond.

The story of Bridgwater's canal basin, now an attractive marina, starts in 1827, when the 14 1/2 mile long Bridgwater and Taunton Canal was opened. Although larger projects to link the Bristol and English Channels by canals and rivers were abandoned, major extensions to Bridgwater Docks were completed in 1841 in response to competition from the newly arrived railway.

Goods traffic, especially coal, continued on the canal until 1907. In the same year the last Bridgwater-built ship, the ketch *Irene*, was launched. Bridgwater Docks finally closed in 1969.

A colourful collection of canal longboats are now moored in the canal basin/marina, where handsome modern buildings blend in well with the remaining industrial architecture of warehouses and chimneys as well as the lock gates and hand cranes. 'Admiral's Landing', an attractive pub in a redeveloped warehouse overlooking the marina, has a very good collection of period photographs showing Bridgwater busy with sailing ships and steamers. Beyond the canal basin, the canal towpath makes a pleasant and surprisingly tranquil walk through town. It continues all the way to Taunton.

Portishead Marina

Portishead's Victorian deep water dock, originally built to accommodate ships too big to reach Bristol Harbour, is the centre of a modern marina. Filled with an array of yachts and surrounded by tall, imaginatively designed apartment buildings in place of the old power stations, the marina was opened in 2001 and was still being developed at the time of writing. It has a bold and decidedly upmarket appearance, heightened by a scattering of modern sculptures, and is entered from the Bristol Channel by way of impressive hydraulically operated lock gates.

Walk from the Marina towards the Pier (unfortunately closed) for a fine view of Avonmouth Docks and the Severn Bridges. Follow the walkway left from the Pier and up steps to the Royal Hotel for an even better view.

Portishead Marina

Some other Bossiney books you may find useful

Exmoor – a Shortish Guide

Shortish Walks on Exmoor (6-9 km)

Shortish Walks – Quantocks and Mendips (6-8 km)

Shortish Walks near Taunton (5-9 km)

Shortish Walks – the Levels and South Somerset (6-8 km)

Really Short walks – Exmoor and Brendon (3-6 km)

Tourist Information Centres

Bridgwater   01278 436438

Burnham-on-Sea   01278 787852

Clevedon   01934 426020

Dunster   01643 821835

Minehead   01643 702624

Porlock   01643 863150

Watchet   01984 632101

Weston-super-Mare   01934 888877